P9-DYA-184

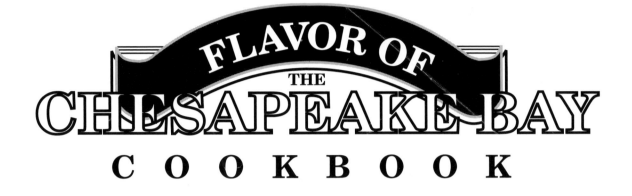

# FLAVOR OF THE CHESAPEAKE BAY COOKBOOK

## Whitey Schmidt

Marian Hartnett Press

Printed in the
United States of America
First Printing 1993
ISBN 0-9613008-7-6

Library of Congress Catalog Number 93-77558
Copyright 1993 by Marian Hartnett Press
Box 88
Crisfield, Maryland 21817

All rights reserved.
No part of this book may be reproduced in any manner whatsoever
without written permission except in the case of brief quotations
embodied in critical articles and reviews.

# CHESAPEAKE BAY

## Photographs
## by
## MARION E. WARREN

# *Introduction*

As far back as I can remember, I was fascinated by the sights, sounds, and smells of the kitchen. My mother always encouraged me to cook. I clearly remember that when I came home late for supper she'd say, "We had dinner hours ago. So if you want something to eat, go fix it yourself." I did. I discovered at an early age that the kitchen was a great place to relax, use your imagination, and, most of all, have fun.

Bay country cuisine is varied and flavorful. I know you'll find preparing these foods is especially enjoyable. Every recipe I've included has been carefully considered and well tested. Dishes were served to guests with discriminating tastes who offered their reactions and suggestions. As a seafood lover myself, I've found writing this book to be a delightful experience.

FLAVOR OF THE CHESAPEAKE BAY COOKBOOK includes 52 remarkable recipes arranged in 5 culinary chapters–Appetizers, Soups, Side Dishes, Main Dishes, and Desserts–to simplify your meal planning. Select one luscious recipe from each section and prepare them. You'll have all the mouth-watering components you'll need for a festive meal that you and your guests will savor and remember.

# Contents

CHAPTER INTRODUCTION PHOTOGRAPHS

*Appetizers*

# OYSTERS ON THE HALF SHELL

**6 oysters**
**2 cups crushed ice**
**1/4 lemon**
**Freshly cracked black pepper**
**Wine vinegar**


Scrub oyster shells under running cold water. Shuck the oysters just before serving and strain the liquor that spills from the shell into a container. Arrange the oysters in their deep shells on a bed of ice, and pour the strained liquor over them. Serve with a wedge of lemon, a bit of cracked pepper, or a splash of vinegar.

*Serves 1.*


***Cocktail Sauce:***
**1 cup chili sauce**
**2 tablespoons prepared horseradish**
**2 tablespoons lemon juice**
**2 tablespoons finely chopped celery**

*The oyster lover demands his oysters pure and undefiled by any other flavor, seasoning, herb, or accompaniment that rivals the briny taste of the Bay. So here is the authentic recipe for savoring oysters, but for those who need more, give this tasty sauce a try.*

*M*ost of the small towns that dot the shores of the Chesapeake owe their existence to the oyster, hence names like Bivalve, Oyster, Oystershell, and Shelltown reflect the Bay's underlying input.

# OYSTERS ROSE HAVEN

**Rock salt**

**8 oysters on the half shell**

**2 tablespoons butter**

**1/4 cup finely chopped fresh spinach**

**2 tablespoons finely chopped parsley**

**2 cloves garlic, crushed**

**1 tablespoon lemon juice**

**4 tablespoons fresh bread crumbs**

**Salt and freshly ground pepper**

Preheat oven to 450 degrees. Fill an oval baking dish with rock salt and arrange the oysters in their half shells on the rock salt. Melt butter and thoroughly blend in spinach, parsley, garlic, lemon juice, bread crumbs, and salt and pepper to taste. Top each oyster with a spoonful of this mixture and bake in the hot oven for 3 to 5 minutes, or until the oysters curl on the edges. Serve immediately.

*Serves 2 to 4.*

*This is another favorite recipe for preparing oysters. Even people who usually don't like oysters will enjoy them if you serve them this way.*

*H*and-tongs become more difficult to
operate as the depth of the water
increases, not to mention balancing
one's self on a constantly  moving boat.

# CAP'N OY

**24 large fresh mushroom caps**

**1/4 cup butter**

**6 green onions, finely chopped**

**1/2 sweet red pepper, sliced julienne style**

**24 small Bay oysters**

**Melted butter**

**Salt**

Saute mushroom crowns gently in the 1/4 cup butter for 3 minutes, stirring carefully so caps do not break. Remove from pan and place on greased cookie sheet, hollow side up. Saute onions and red pepper strips until limp in remaining butter; put about 1/4 teaspoon chopped onion inside each mushroom cap. Dip oysters in melted butter; place an oyster inside each mushroom; sprinkle lightly with salt. Heat under broiler until edges of oysters start to curl. Garnish with red pepper. Serve at once.

*Serves a crowd.*

*There is something comforting about the ease and simplicity of preparing oysters this way. The mushroom itself cradles the succulent oyster as naturally as the oyster shell. We like to call it Neptune's china.*

*The "Carabee" sets a sparkling sail on Whitehall Creek, maneuvering the sharp dog-leg channel around a treacherous shoal. Once past the last red marker, Whitehall Creek reveals a popular and well-protected anchorage.*

# MARYLAND CLAMS CASINO

**1 dozen clams in shells**
**1/4 cup chopped onion**
**1/4 cup chopped green pepper**
**1 tablespoon butter, melted**
**1/4 cup chopped pimento**
**3 slices bacon, cut into fourths**
**Lemon wedges**
**Fresh parsley sprigs**
**Seasoned bread crumbs for topping**

Wash clams. Pry open shells, discard top shells, and loosen meat from bottom shells. Place shells and meat on paper towels to drain thoroughly.

Saute onion and green pepper in butter; stir in chopped pimento. Return clams to shells, and arrange shells in a shallow baking pan. Spoon 1 tablespoon vegetable mixture onto each clam; top with bacon and bread crumbs. Bake at 375 degrees for 15 to 20 minutes or until bacon is browned. Garnish with lemon wedges and parsley sprigs.

*Serves 4.*

*These "do ahead" casinos are your passport to a perfect party. Preparation begins the day before—cover with plastic wrap and refrigerate. When guests arrive, open the wine and pop the casinos into the oven. The results are mighty good.*

*T*he Hammond-Harwood House is a
National Historic Landmark in Annapolis,
Maryland.

14

# OLD FASHIONED EGG NOG

**12 eggs, separated**

**2 cups sugar**

**1 quart milk**

**1 pint heavy cream**

**1/2 cup rum**

**1 pint rye whiskey**

**Garnish: freshly grated nutmeg**

Separate eggs. Beat yolks and whites separately. Beat whites until frothy. Add 1 cup sugar to yolks and 1 cup sugar to whites. Beat again. Combine eggs and sugar together. Add milk, cream, rum, and whiskey. Serve with freshly grated nutmeg as garnish.

Chill 2 hours. The longer it chills, the stronger it gets. I often make it the night before.

*It's December, and visions of sugarplums inspire us in our annual quest for the perfect holiday appetizer. These are the foods memories are made of. Here is the kick with this recipe—vary the liquors as you will. Some folks prefer rye whiskey or different ratios of bourbon whiskey to rum. Keep trying until you get it right!*

15

*W*elcome to Crisfield, Maryland, the "Crab Capital of the World." Here, the oysters are succulent, the clams plump and juicy, and the crabs grow big and blue.

# CRABTOWNE CRAB DIP

1/2 cup green pepper, minced

2 tablespoons unsalted butter

12 ounces cream cheese, softened

1/4 cup mayonnaise

1 tablespoon capers, minced and drained

Dry white wine

1 tablespoon horseradish

2 teaspoons Worcestershire sauce

1 teaspoon lemon rind, minced

Tabasco sauce

Salt, to taste

Black pepper

1 pound crab meat

Bread crumbs

Preheat oven to 350 degrees. In a skillet, cook green pepper in butter over moderate heat for 3 minutes. In a ceramic bowl, combine green peppers with cream cheese, mayonnaise, capers, wine, horseradish, Worcestershire sauce, lemon rind, Tabasco sauce, and seasonings. Fold in crab meat. Transfer to 1-quart baking dish. Sprinkle with bread crumbs and bake until bubbly.

*There are as many variations of creamy crab dip as there are day trips through Bay country history. Each trip takes a different turn with a new perspective. This dip takes on special meaning with a splash of sherry.*

*Queens Creek on the Piankatank River, a quiet world of scenic beauty.*

18

# THE KING'S CRAB TREATS

**1 egg**

**4 tablespoons mayonnaise**

**1-1/2 tablespoons prepared yellow mustard**

**1 pound backfin crab meat**

**4 slices white bread**

**1 tablespoon celery salt**

**1 teaspoon seafood seasoning**

**Dash pepper**

**2 tablespoons chopped fresh parsley**

**Peanut oil**

In a bowl, mix egg, mayonnaise, and mustard. Add crab meat, and carefully toss until blended. Whip bread in blender to make crumbs and add to it the celery salt, seafood seasoning, pepper, and parsley. Add bread mixture to crab meat mixture. Form into 30 small balls and deep fry in peanut oil heated to 350 degrees until golden brown.

*Serves 6 to 8.*

*You don't need royalty to enjoy this tasty treat, but if you have a prince or princess you want to impress, be sure to prepare a double batch. Like the king's gold, they disappear quickly,*

19

*Soups*

# Back Creek Bean Soup

1 pound navy beans, soaked overnight

1 1- to 2-pound meaty ham bone

1 large onion, diced

2 tablespoons olive oil

1 sweet green pepper, diced

1 sweet red pepper, diced

1 celery rib, diced

Salt and freshly ground black pepper

Dash of cayenne

Drain the beans and place in a soup pot. Add the ham bone and enough fresh water to cover the beans by 1 inch.

In a separate fry pan over low heat, soften the onion in the oil for about 5 minutes. Add the peppers and celery and cook for another 5 minutes. Add the vegetables to the beans and ham.

Simmer the soup for 45 to 60 minutes, until the beans are done. Remove the ham bone from the soup and let it cool. Puree about half of the soup and return it to the pot. Cut the meat from the ham bone and add it to the soup. Season the soup with salt, pepper, and cayenne. Serve hot.

*Serves 6 to 8.*

*If you don't have time to soak the beans overnight, cover them with 3 inches of water and bring to a boil. Simmer for 5 minutes, covered, then remove from the heat and let the beans soak in the cooking liquid for 1 to 2 hours. This is a soup that always tastes better the day after it's prepared.*

*Southern Maryland, some of the most fertile farmland in America, is borderded by the Potomac River on the west, the Patuxent River on the east, and is fronted by the majestic Chesapeake Bay. Farms like this abound in Bay country; they often stretch from the main house to the waters' edge.*

# SETTLERS' SOUP

**2 to 3 pounds meaty soup bones**
**8 cups water**
**3 teaspoons salt**
**1/4 teaspoon thyme leaves, minced**
**1/4 teaspoon pepper**
**2 whole allspice**
**2 cubes beef bouillon**
**1 bay leaf**
**2 medium potatoes, peeled and cubed**
**2 stalks celery, sliced**
**2 medium carrots, sliced**
**1 large onion, chopped**
**2 cups tomatoes, chopped**
**1-1/2 cups whole kernel corn**

In large soup pot, combine soup bones, water, salt, thyme, pepper, allspice, bouillon, and bay leaf. Simmer, covered, 1-1/2 to 3 hours or until meat is tender. Remove soup bones, allspice, and bay leaf. Cut meat from bones and return to soup. Add remaining ingredients; simmer covered for 30 minutes or until vegetables are tender. Correct seasoning.

*Serves 6.*

*Soup was one of the mainstays of the early settlers' diets. This recipe is typical of the soups served in country villages when stock pots were kept going on the back of the stove and when the settlers' own gardens provide the vegetables.*

23

*The rivers of the Chesapeake Bay were a busy place in steamboat days. Freight and passenger steamers connected the small towns that lined the shores. Many of those towns no longer have docks to receive passengers. Here, a lone heron searches for a meal under a dilapidated dock.*

# STEAMBOAT STEW

**3 large onions, chopped**
**1/2 cup olive oil**
**1 quart water**
**2 cups dry red or white wine**
**2 10-ounce cans tomato paste**
**1 tablespoon sugar**
**1 tablespoon salt**
**1 teaspoon oregano**
**1 teaspoon basil**
**1 teaspoon pepper**
**1/2 cup parsley flakes**
**1 pound skinless fish fillets**
**1 pound crab meat**
**1 dozen soft shell clams**
**1 dozen cherrystone clams**
**1 dozen oysters**

In a large pan, saute onions in oil until tender. Add water, wine, tomato paste, and seasonings. Simmer, covered, for 1 hour. Wash fish fillets and cut into pieces. Remove any shell from crab meat. Scrub clams and oyster shells well with a brush. Add the shellfish to the broth first and cook for 20 to 30 minutes, or until the shells open. Then add the fish and cook another 6 to 10 minutes.

*Serves 8 to 10.*

*There are as many variations of this stew as there are fish in the Bay; each time this dish is prepared it is different. The beauty of it is that you can go to the market with an open mind and select the freshest and best-looking seafood you find there, but you should feel free to substitute or add others. besides shellfish.*

25

*In the blue stillness of morning at Smith Island, this waterman eyes the horizon. A lone sunbeam breaks the greyness, creating endless ripples on the water.*

# Chancellor's Point Clam Chowder

1/4 pound salt pork
1 onion, finely chopped
2 potatoes; peeled, sliced, and coarsely chopped
1 cup water
1 cup clam juice
1 quart fresh clams, coarsely chopped
1 cup milk
1 cup heavy cream
Salt and freshly ground pepper
1 tablespoon sweet butter
Oyster crackers

Cut the salt pork into small cubes and render them in a heavy kettle. Remove the cracklings and saute onion until golden brown. Add potatoes, water, clam juice, and bring to a boil. Reduce heat and simmer for 10 minutes. Add the clams with their natural liquid and simmer for another 10 minutes. Scald the milk and the heavy cream in a pot and pour into the kettle with the clam mixture. Season with salt and pepper and simmer for 30 minutes. Just before serving, add the butter. Serve piping hot and pass crisp oyster crackers for a topping.

*Serves 6 to 8.*

*Clam chowder is one of the earliest and most famous of the seafood stews from Bay country. Potatoes found their way into clam chowder in the 18th century, but salt pork and onions were ingredients from the beginning.*

*Crab pots are constantly in need of repair.*

# CORN AND CRAB BISQUE

**3 ounces bacon**
**1/2 onion, finely chopped**
**1/2 cup chopped celery**
**1/2 green pepper, finely chopped**
**1/2 red pepper, finely chopped**
**1/2 cup raw, peeled, finely diced potatoes**
**3 cups water**
**1/4 teaspoon paprika**
**Bay leaf**
**3 tablespoons flour**
**2 cups milk**
**2 cups cooked Silver Queen corn**
**1/2 pound crab meat**
**Garnish: fresh parsley**

Saute the bacon until very crisp. Remove and crumble. In the bacon drippings, saute onion, celery, and peppers until onion is soft, but not brown. Add the water, bay leaf, paprika, and potatoes and simmer until the potatoes are tender (35 to 40 minutes).

Bring just to the boiling point and add the flour and 1/2 cup of the milk.

In a separate saucepan, heat crab meat, corn, and the remaining milk. When warmed through (but not boiling), add this and the bacon to the soup mixture. Heat gently for a few minutes. Garnish with fresh parsley.

*Serves 6.*

*If the bisque turns out too thick for your liking, a little milk can be added to thin out the consistency. If, on the other hand, the soup turns out too thin for your tastes, simply uncover the pot and simmer the soup base 15 minutes or so longer.*

*A crabber's dictionary describes a "peeler" as a crab about to shed.*

30

# SHE CRAB SOUP

**1 pound lump crab meat**
**1/4 cup grated onion**
**1 medium carrot, grated**
**2 tablespoons unsalted butter**
**2 tablespoons all-purpose flour**
**2 cups chicken broth**
**2 cups half-and-half**
**1 tablespoon dry sherry**
**1 or 2 dashes of Tabasco**
**Salt**
**Garnish: chopped parsley**

Remove any shell from the crab meat and set aside. In a soup pot, soften the onion and carrot in the butter over low heat. After the vegetables have cooked for about 10 minutes, sprinkle them with the flour and cook for about 5 minutes, being careful the flour does not brown.

Stir in the chicken broth and the half-and-half. Add the sherry and Tabasco. Cook, stirring occasionally, for about 10 minutes. Add the crab meat and heat thoroughly for about 5 minutes. Adjust the seasoning.

Serve the soup garnished with the chopped parsley and pass sherry for additional flavor.

*Serves 4 to 6.*

*Authentic she crab soup is made with female blue crabs because the fat and orange egg paste is used to flavor the base. When female crabs are not available, regular crab meat is used and diced carrots added in place of the fat and egg paste.*

31

*H*ere a waterman loads oysters into bushel baskets. The day's catch is kept under refrigeration until it reaches the cook's preparation table in Kent Narrows, Maryland.

# Oyster Stew

**24 fresh oysters, shucked, liquor reserved**

**1 tablespoon fresh thyme**

**1/2 teaspoon celery salt**

**Pinch cayenne pepper**

**2 cups heavy cream**

**2 cups milk**

**4 tablespoons sweet butter, cut in small pieces**

**Salt and pepper to taste**

**1/4 cup chopped fresh parsley**

In a large saucepan, heat oyster liquor with thyme, celery salt, and cayenne. Add oysters and cook until their edges just begin to curl. Add cream, milk, and butter. Heat slowly, stirring gently; do not boil. Season with salt and pepper. Add chopped parsley and serve in warm soup bowls.

*Serves 4.*

*Indians supplied the settlers with oysters. The Indians preferred to eat their oysters cooked and, perhaps, they shared their recipe for oyster stew with the colonists. Huge mounds of oyster shells have been found along the shores of the Chesapeake Bay. The heavy cream is a modern addition to this recipe.*

*A* *trotline is a long line, resting on the*
*Bay's bottom and anchored at both ends, to*
*which a series of baits are tied at 3-foot*
*intervals and worked from a boat.*
*Commercial crabbers of the Severn River*
*near Annapolis, Maryland run one, two, or*
*three lines up to a mile in length.*

34

# MARYLAND STYLE CRAB SOUP

**4 cups cold water**
**1 cup diced carrots**
**1 cup chopped onion**
**3/4 cup chopped celery**
**1/4 cup butter**
**1 tablespoon seafood seasoning**
**1 tablespoon Worcestershire sauce**
**1-1/2 cups diced potatoes**
**1 cup chopped cabbage**
**1 1-pound can tomatoes, chopped**
**2 tablespoons parsley**
**1 tablespoon flour (mixed with 1/3 cup water to thicken)**
**1 pound Maryland crab meat**
**Salt and pepper**

Put water in large pot and bring to a boil. Add all ingredients except crab meat and flour mixture. Bring to boil, then simmer 1-1/2 hours. Thicken with flour mixture. Add crab meat, simmer 1/2 hour. Yields 1-1/2 quarts. Salt and pepper to taste.

*Serves 6 to 8.*

*Want a great way to warm up on a cold winter's night? You whip up a pot of this...serve it with a stack of buttered saltine crackers...top it off with a fine bottle of white wine...and throw another log on the fire! Now that's Bay country.*

*A tradition in the 1870's called "pea-parchings" was held in the peanut fields after the crop was dug. A shock of peanut vines, reserved for the children, would be burned and the children were allowed to recover the roasted peanuts from the embers.*

36

# SURRY COUNTY CREAM OF PEANUT SOUP

1 medium-size onion, finely chopped

1/2 cup finely chopped celery

4 tablespoons butter

4 tablespoons flour

2 quarts chicken broth

1 cup smooth peanut butter

2 cups half-and-half

Salt to taste

Black pepper to taste

Chopped peanuts for garnish


In a large skillet, saute onion and celery in butter until soft, but not browned. Add flour and stir well. Pour in 1 cup chicken broth and bring mixture to a boil, stirring frequently. Remove mixture from heat and place 1/2 cup at a time in a blender or food processor. Blend until smooth. Return blended mixture to skillet and add remaining chicken broth, half-and-half, and peanut butter. Whisk while heating gently. Do not allow mixture to boil. Season to taste with salt and pepper. Serve hot or cold, garnished with chopped peanuts.

*Serves 8.*

*Peanuts came to Virginia with slaves from Africa soon after the settlement of Jamestown. It was along the James River during the Civil War that Union soldiers for the first time discovered edibles called "goobers," or "ground nuts." The rest is history.*

37

*Side Dishes*

# HOLLAND POINT HUSH PUPPIES

1/2 cup all-purpose flour

1 tablespoon light brown sugar

1/8 teaspoon salt

2 tablespoons baking powder

1/2 teaspoon baking soda

1-1/2 cups yellow cornmeal

1 egg

1 cup buttermilk

1 onion, finely chopped

Bacon drippings and peanut oil for frying

In a large bowl, combine flour, sugar, salt, baking powder, and baking soda. Mix well. Stir in cornmeal. Add egg and beat mixture with a wooden spoon until smooth. Pour in buttermilk and stir until absorbed. Stir in onion. In a deep skillet, heat bacon drippings until very hot—375 degrees on a deep-frying thermometer. Add peanut oil to a depth of 2 to 3 inches in skillet. Drop hush puppies by teaspoonfuls into oil. Fry, turning once, until golden on all sides, about 3 minutes each. Drain on paper towels. Serve warm with butter.

*Serves 12.*

*Deep-fried hush puppies are served with fried fish throughout Bay country. The secret in this recipe is to not fry perfectly rounded teaspoonfuls of the puppies but whatever shapes they fall into when dropped into the oil.*

*Southern Maryland member of the Piscataway Indian Tribe.*

40

# INDIAN CORN PUDDING

**2 cups thin cream**

**2 cups fresh corn**

**2 tablespoons melted butter**

**2 tablespoons sugar**

**1 teaspoon salt**

**1/4 teaspoon pepper**

**3 eggs, well beaten**

Add the cream, corn, butter, sugar, and seasonings to the eggs. Pour into a well-greased casserole and bake in a moderate oven for about 45 minutes or until the pudding is set. Insert a knife into the center of the pudding and, if it comes out clean, the pudding is done. For variety, add 1/4 cup chopped green peppers or pimento or 1/2 cup minced ham or chopped mushrooms.

*Serves 6 to 8.*

*Corn has been a valuable food throughout the history of Bay country. From the American Indians, corn recipes found their way to many Chesapeake kitchens. Early settlers planned their arrival in spring so they could plant corn and other crops to tide them through the following season.*

*Throngs of people stop at roadside fruit and vegetable stands on summer week-ends. The sight of glossy green peppers, deep red tomatoes, potatoes still with dirt on the skins, crisp sugar peas, and just-picked peaches is immensely satisfying, particularly if the stand happens to be on the edge of an orchard or field of corn.*

# TIDEWATER TATER SALAD

8 medium potatoes
Salted water to cover
4 stalks celery, chopped
1 small yellow onion, finely chopped
5 green onions, minced
1/2 cup green bell pepper, diced
1 tablespoons dry mustard
1/2 teaspoon Tabasco sauce
1 cup mayonnaise
1/3 pound Virginia ham, diced
1 pound backfin crab meat
Salt and black pepper to taste

Put potatoes in a large pot, add salted water to cover, and bring
to a boil. Cook until just tender. Test with a fork and drain. Peel
off skins while potatoes are still somewhat hot. Cut into desired-
size pieces for salad and let cool. In a small bowl, combine celery,
yellow and green onions, bell pepper, mustard, Tabasco, and
mayonnaise. Mix well. In a separate large bowl, combine potatoes, crab meat, and ham. Add mayonnaise mixture, salt and
pepper to taste, and toss very gently so as not to break up crab
meat.

*Serves 10.*

*Potatoes are a traditional accompaniment
for many backyard picnics. They can be
wrapped in foil and tossed on the grill or, as
they are done here, cooked and prepared
with salty Virginia ham and chunks of lump
crab meat—mmmm good.*

*This scarecrow is set up in a field to scare birds away from crops. It silently stands guard over this lower shore garden patch.*

44

# OLD-FASHIONED POTATO SALAD

1 large celery rib, diced
1/4 cup diced onion
1 small sweet green pepper, diced
2 hard-cooked eggs, diced
1/2 cup mayonnaise
1 teaspoon sugar
Salt and freshly ground black pepper
1-1/2 pounds new potatoes, scrubbed and cut into bite-size
   pieces

*Vinaigrette:*
2 tablespoons olive oil
1 tablespoon cider vinegar
2 teaspoons fresh chopped basil
1/2 teaspoon fresh, chopped thyme
1/2 teaspoon salt
Freshly ground black pepper


Steam or boil the potatoes just until tender. Drain and let cool slightly. Mix the vinaigrette ingredients together in a small bowl. Place the potatoes in a bowl and pour the vinaigrette over them.

Add the diced vegetables and toss gently. Add the eggs, mayonnaise, and sugar. Season the salad with salt and pepper and toss gently. Refrigerate for at least an hour before serving; adjust the seasonings just before serving.

*Serves 8.*

*This recipe represents the classic dish, preserving the spirit and flavor of this aromatic salad in an uncomplicated, accessible way. Backyard party-goers are often captivated at the first taste. Potato salad is a versatile dish, too. Serve it for lunch or dinner.*

*T*he roaring motors of the workboat are a loud contrast to the quiet islands that many watermen call home. Rhodes Point, Maryland.

# BUTTERMILK CORN BREAD

**2 tablespoons bacon drippings or butter**

**1-1/2 cups yellow cornmeal**

**1-1/2 teaspoons baking powder**

**3 tablespoons flour**

**1/2 teaspoon salt**

**2 tablespoons molasses**

**1-1/2 cups buttermilk**

**1 egg**

Preheat oven to 450 degrees. Melt bacon drippings or butter in a heavy 9-inch, cast-iron skillet. In a mixing bowl, combine cornmeal, flour, salt, and baking powder. Add buttermilk and egg. Mix well. Add melted butter and molasses and stir to blend. Pour batter into hot skillet. Place skillet in oven and bake for 20 to 25 minutes, or until golden brown. Serve warm with butter.

*Serves 6.*

*Indians made their corn bread by grinding corn, mixing it with water, and baking it in a cake-like patty over an open fire. Although this bread can be made in a baking dish, for a more traditional version, bake it in a cast-iron skillet.*

*S*un-up to sun-down, these watermen ply
the waters near Wye Island, Maryland in
search of tasty blue crabs.

# OYSTER AND CRAB FRITTERS

**1 pint oysters and liquor**
**Corn flake crumbs**
**2 eggs**
**1/2 cup milk**
**1 teaspoon lemon zest, grated**
**3/4 cup all-purpose flour**
**1 teaspoon baking powder**
**1 teaspoon salt**
**1/2 pound crab meat**
**Oil for frying**

*Curry Sauce:*
**1-1/2 cups dry white wine**
**2 tablespoons oyster liquor**
**1/4 teaspoon curry powder**
**1-1/2 tablespoons cornstarch**
**3 tablespoons cream**
**Freshly ground white pepper**

Drain the oysters, cut them into quarters, and roll them in corn flake crumbs. Reserve 2 tablespoons of the liquor for the sauce. Simmer the wine, oyster liquor, and curry in an uncovered saucepan for 15 minutes. Combine the cornstarch and cream; add them to the wine, and heat, stirring constantly, until the mixture thickens. Season to taste with pepper and keep the sauce warm. Separate the eggs and whisk the yolks, milk, and lemon zest in a bowl. Sift the flour, baking powder, and salt together, and add them to the eggs, mixing well. Add the crab meat and stir it into the batter. Add a pinch of salt to the egg whites and whip until stiff. Stir 2 tablespoons into the batter; fold in the remaining whites and oysters.

Heat a skillet until a drop of water sizzles on the surface, brush lightly with oil. Cook four fritters at one time, measuring the amount of batter with a large spoon. Turn once to brown both sides evenly. Serve immediately with the hot curry sauce.

*Serves 6 to 8.*

*This is a delightful recipe that combines two of my favorite foods and two separate methods of preparation. If you choose not to skillet fry, an alternative method is deep frying with equally good, but different, results.*

*H*istory flows in the deep amber waters of the Pocomoke River. Local tradition says that the word "Pocomoke" is an Indian word that means "black water." More than 27 species of mammals, 29 of reptiles, 49 of amphibians, and 172 species of birds have been seen in the wetlands bordering the river.

50

# SNOW HILL BAKED BEANS

2 cups navy beans

8 cups water

1/2 pound salt pork, cut into 1/2-inch pieces

2 tablespoons packed brown sugar

1/2 teaspoon salt

1/2 teaspoon dry mustard

1 small onion, chopped

1/2 cup molasses

1/4 cup chili sauce


In large saucepan, cover beans with water. Soak overnight or about 12 hours. Heat beans and soaking water to boiling. Simmer covered, about 1 hour or until beans are almost tender. Drain; reserve liquid.

Heat oven to 300 degrees. In bean pot or large casserole, combine beans and salt pork. Add enough water to reserved bean liquid to measure 2 cups. Stir remaining ingredients into 2 cups bean liquid. Pour over beans; mix gently. Bake covered at 300 degrees for 6 to 7 hours, stirring occasionally; add water, if necessary. Remove cover during last hour of baking and bake without stirring.

*Serves 6 to 8.*

*No picnic or fishing party is complete without baked beans and this delicious recipe is one you will try again and again.*

51

*The Bay is changing and yet the Bay has never really changed. After centuries, it is still as an early sailor described it, "The noblest Bay in the universe."*

# Savory Green Beans
# With New Potatoes

**1-1/2 pounds fresh green beans**

**6 cups water**

**1/4 pound diced salt pork or ham hock**

**Salt to taste**

**Dash sugar**

**1 teaspoon fresh summer savory**

**1 pound small new potatoes, pared**

String the beans, cut into 1 1/2-inch pieces, and wash. Put water in a 3-quart saucepan and add diced salt pork or ham hock. Cover and cook about 20 minutes. Add beans, salt, sugar, and summer savory. Cook about 20 minutes. Place pared potatoes on top of beans and continue cooking until potatoes are tender.

*Serves 6.*

*Backyard beans with shore potatoes, serve me some with sliced tomatoes. This dish gets extra added attention from the addition of peppery summer savory. See if you don't agree.*

*Main Dishes*

# SMITH ISLAND SEAFOOD SOUFFLE

**1 cup backfin crab meat**
**1/2 cup finely diced Smithfield ham**
**1/2 cup peeled, chopped steamed shrimp**
**3 tablespoons butter**
**3 tablespoons flour**
**1 cup milk**
**2 tablespoons dry sherry**
**4 egg yolk**
**Salt, black pepper, and ground nutmeg to taste**
**1/4 teaspoon Tabasco sauce**
**2/3 cup grated Swiss cheese**
**6 egg whites**

Preheat oven to 375 degrees.

In a bowl, toss together the crab meat, ham, and shrimp. Set aside.

In an enamel pan, melt the butter and whisk in the flour. Cook 2 minutes, stirring constantly. Do not brown the flour.

Off the heat, gradually whisk in the milk and sherry. Return to the heat and bring almost to a boil, stirring all the while. Beat in the egg yolks, one at a time. Season well with salt, pepper, and nutmeg. Stir in the Tabasco and all but 3 tablespoons of the cheese. Gently fold in crab meat mixture. Beat the egg whites until stiff peaks form and gently fold into souffle mixture.

Butter a 2-quart souffle dish and sprinkle the reserved cheese on the bottom. Pour in the souffle mixture and bake about 30 minutes, or until nicely browned and firm. Serve at once.

*Serves 4.*

*One thing you must do when preparing this recipe is to have your guests seated at the table. Then remove the souffle from the oven (careful, it's hot) and proceed directly to the table. Don't delay, serve at once.*

55

*We* have many fond memories of Sunday afternoons feasting on stuffed ham at the church suppers.

56

# SOUTHERN MARYLAND STUFFED HAM

**1 10- to 12-pound fully-cooked ham**
**3 pounds kale**
**3 pounds cabbage**
**2 pounds yellow onions**
**1 pound scallions**
**2 tablespoons celery seed**
**2 tablespoons mustard seed**
**1-1/2 tablespoons salt**
**1 tablespoon freshly ground black pepper**
**1/4 cup cayenne, or more to taste**

Trim the ham of the rind and most of the fat. Chop the kale into small pieces. Chop the cabbage into small pieces. Blanch the kale and cabbage in boiling water for 5 minutes. Refresh under cold running water and drain in a colander set over a large bowl. Press well, but do not squeeze, to extract excess liquid. Reserve the liquid.

Peel and trim the yellow onions and fine-dice them. Trim the scallions, leaving about 6 inches of green, and slice them cross-wise. Mix all the vegetables together in a large bowl. Add the celery seed, mustard seed, salt, black pepper, and cayenne.

Make deep slits in the ham with a thin, narrow knife. The cuts should be made perpendicular to the bone, so that the ham shows a nice pattern when it is sliced. Pack the ham with the stuffing, pushing it into each cut to pack as fully as possible. Cover the ham with the remaining stuffing. To prepare for cooking, wrap the ham in a large piece of cheesecloth. Tie securely with a piece of string or kitchen twine.

Place a rack in a large pot. Lower the ham into the pot, then add the reserved vegetable liquor and hot water to cover. Bring to a boil. Reduce the heat to a simmer. Cover the pot and cook for 20 minutes per pound.

Cool the ham in its liquor. Remove the ham and wrap it with foil, then refrigerate. Carve in paper-thin slices, and serve cold.

*Serves 10 to 16.*

57

*The Amish population is well represented around Bay country, as shown in this photograph of an Amish farm at sunrise.*

# CHICKEN IN THE POT

1 chicken, about 4 pounds
Soup bone, veal knuckle
2 carrots, sliced
2 leeks, sliced
2 celery stalks, sliced
1 onion stuck with a clove
3 sprigs parsley
1 bay leaf
5 peppercorns
1 teaspoon salt
6 cups water
2 cups chicken broth
1 cup green peas
1 cup cooked, wide noodles
Freshly chopped parsley

Put chicken in a large kettle. Add the veal knuckle, carrots, leeks, celery, onion, parsley, bay leaf, peppercorns, salt, water, and chicken broth. Bring slowly to a boil. Reduce the heat and simmer for about 1-1/2 to 2 hours.

Remove the parsley and bay leaf. Add the peas and simmer for another 5 minutes. Add the noodles and heat through. To serve, remove the soup bone. Take the chicken out and cut into serving-size pieces. Put the chicken pieces in a large earthenware casserole and pour the contents of the kettle over them. Sprinkle with parsley.

*Serves 6.*

*Mom says that chicken soup is the universal cure-all for just about everything. I do believe that there is something soothing, loving, and warming about it. Give it a try.*

*"Winter on Spa Creek"* as the Maryland State Capital Building looms in the background.

# CHICKEN POT PIE

**Pie Filling:**
**4 chicken breasts**
**1-1/2 quarts water**
**2 ounces white wine**
**1/2 teaspoon rosemary**
**1 clove garlic, crushed**
**2 bay leaves**
**1/2 teaspoon thyme**
**1/4 teaspoon tarragon**
**4 whole black peppercorns**
**4 tablespoons butter**
**4 tablespoons flour**
**24 pearl onions**
**1 cup peas**
**2 carrots, peeled and diced**

**Biscuit Topping:**
**3-1/2 cups all-purpose flour**
**1 tablespoon plus 1 teaspoon baking powder**
**Good pinch salt**
**7 tablespoons butter**
**1-1/4 cups buttermilk**
**Egg wash (1 whole egg and 1 tablespoon water beaten until frothy)**
**Melted butter**

To prepare the filling, combine the chicken, water, wine, garlic, herbs and peppercorns in a large saucepan and bring to the boil. Skim the top and reduce the heat. Allow to simmer 20 to 30 minutes, or until the chicken is tender. Remove the chicken from the pot and allow it to cool. Skin and remove the meat from the bone. Return the bones to the stock. Simmer the stock until reduced by half. Strain the stock and bring back to the boil. Blend 4 tablespoons of butter and 4 table-spoons of flour and cook over low heat for 5 minutes without brown-ing. Beat the stock gradually into this mixture. Simmer for 10 minutes. Cook the peas, carrots, and onions in separate pots of boil-ing water until tender. Dice the chicken and combine with all the remaining ingredients. Put in individual crocks.

Meanwhile, prepare the biscuits. Preheat the oven to 400 degrees and combine all the dry ingredients in a bowl. Cut in the butter until the mixture has the consistency of small peas. Add the buttermilk, stirring in gradually. On a floured board, roll out the dough about 1/2 to 3/4-inch thick. Cut with a floured biscuit cutter and brush each round with the egg wash. Bake for 25 to 30 minutes, or until golden brown. When the biscuits are removed from the oven, brush with melted butter. Place one biscuit on top of each crock of chicken filling. Cook through in the oven until piping hot and serve immediately.

*Serves 8.*

*T*his Paul Bunyan-size frying pan, more
than 10 feet in diameter, is used to prepare
hundreds of pounds of chicken at the
annual Delmarva Chicken Festival, sponsored by Delmarva Poultry Industry, Inc.,
as a means of spotlighting its multi-million
dollar poultry industry.

62

# Maryland Fried Chicken With Gravy

**3- to 3 1/2-pound frying chicken, cut into serving pieces**
**6 slices bacon**
**Vegetable oil for frying**
**3/4 cup flour**
**1 teaspoon salt**
**1/4 teaspoon black pepper**
**2 tablespoons flour**
**1 cup milk**
**1 cup heavy cream**

In a large skillet, fry bacon until browned. Remove bacon and drain on paper towels. Add enough vegetable oil to bacon drippings to make a 1-inch deep layer in skillet. Place 3/4 cup flour, salt, and black pepper in a large plastic or paper bag. Shake well to blend. Coat each chicken piece in flour mixture by placing in bag and shaking. Heat fat in skillet. When bubbling hot, add chicken pieces and fry, turning occasionally, until nicely browned on all sides. Cover skillet, reduce heat, and cook over a low heat for about 25 minutes, or until tender when tested with a fork. Remove chicken, set aside and keep warm. Drain all but 4 tablespoons of fat from skillet. Stir 2 tablespoons of flour and cook for about 3 minutes. Add milk and cream. Continue cooking, stirring occasionally, until gravy is thick and smooth. Add salt and pepper to taste. Pour gravy over hot chicken and garnish with bacon strips.

*Serves 4.*

*Nothing-but-nothing beats a good plate of crispy fried chicken, and this recipe is hard to beat because it's loaded with all the good things that Marylanders love to eat. Young spring chicken pieces are rolled in seasoned flour and fried in a heavy skillet. The cream gravy, made in the same skillet, is poured over the chicken.*

*A*round Bay country, oysters are graded by their size. "Counts" and "extra-selects" are the largest. "Selects" are medium in size and are commonly used in frying. Smaller "standards" are often used in soups and stews.

# CRUSTY COUNTRY FRIED OYSTERS

**2 eggs, beaten**
**3 tablespoons cold water**
**1 pint fresh select oysters, drained**
**1-1/2 cups saltine cracker crumbs**
**Vegetable oil**

Combine eggs and water. Dip oysters in egg mixture and roll each in cracker crumbs. Fry in hot oil (375 degrees) about 2 minutes, or until golden brown, turning to brown both sides. Drain on paper towels.

*Serves 4.*

***Tartar Sauce:***
**1 cup mayonnaise**
**3 tablespoons minced sweet pickles**
**1 minced shallot**
**2 tablespoons snipped chives**
**2 tablespoons minced parsley**
**1 tablespoon minced fresh tarragon**
**1 tablespoon capers**
**Dijon mustard**
**White wine vinegar**

Combine all and refrigerate to blend flavor. Serve with oysters.

*Oysters, pearls of the Bay, take on a special flavor when prepared using this wonderful recipe. It's my favorite. Once you try it, it will be yours, too.*

*Car headlights form streaks over the moon-lit bridge. "I stood on top of the old ferry terminal when I took this photo." (M. Warren)*

# SCALLOPED OYSTERS

24 large oysters
8 tablespoons unsalted butter
1 garlic clove
1 cup fresh bread crumbs
2 tablespoons finely chopped parsley
1 tablespoon finely chopped fresh dill
1 tablespoon finely chopped fresh marjoram
1 tablespoon finely chopped fresh basil
Salt and freshly ground pepper
1/4 cup heavy cream
Lemon wedges

Remove the oysters from their shells and pat them dry; strain and reserve 1/4 cup of the liquor. Melt 4 tablespoons of butter in a saucepan and saute the garlic until it is tender, and discard the garlic. Stir in the bread crumbs and parsley. Blend the remaining butter with the remaining herbs. Add a dash of salt and pepper to the butter. Sprinkle half the crumbs on the bottom of a 9 x 9-inch casserole. Arrange the oysters in a single layer, sprinkle with oyster liquor, and dot with the herb butter. Cover with the remaining crumbs and drizzle with cream. Bake for 15 minutes at 375 degrees until the top is golden brown and bubbling. Serve immediately with a small tray of lemon wedges.

*Serves 4.*

*When the meal must be extra special, this is the special dish you want to serve. Loaded with fresh herbs and chock full of rich, creamy taste, this is one casserole that your family will want you to make over and over again. And it's easy, too!*

67

*T*his photograph, taken on Tilghman Island, clearly shows the hand-tongs used to gather oysters. This waterman is shoveling oysters from piles on the deck into bushel baskets.

# TILGHMAN BAKED OYSTERS

**24 oysters**
**Sweet bell pepper sauce**
**6 pieces bacon, cut into 2-inch squares**
**Rock salt**

Preheat oven to 450 degrees. Shuck the oysters, keeping the oyster meat in the deep part of the shell. On each oyster, place about 1 tablespoon of the sweet pepper sauce. Top with a bacon piece.

On a heat-proof tray, make a layer of rock salt and arrange the oysters on it. Bake 6 to 8 minutes, or until oysters begin to curl at edges and bacon begins to brown slightly.

*Serves 4 to 6.*


***Sweet Bell Pepper Sauce:***
**1 large red bell pepper**
**6 tablespoons unsalted butter**
**1 small onion, coarsely chopped**
**1/4 cup heavy cream**
**Salt and freshly ground black pepper**

Roast the red pepper: Under a broiler or over the open flame of a gas burner or grill, blister the skin of the pepper all over (it should be quite thoroughly black). Place the pepper in a paper bag for 15 minutes to cool and steam. Remove the pepper, cut off the stem and seeds, and scrape off all the skin with the blunt side of a knife. Do not rinse the pepper; the few charred bits that may remain will not hurt. Chop the pepper and set aside. You should have about 1/2 cup.

In a small saucepan, melt the butter and saute the onion until translucent. Remove from heat and allow to cool a bit. Put the red pepper, butter, and sauteed onion in a blender or food processor and puree until smooth. Scrape the pureed pepper back into the saucepan. Add the cream and heat gently. Do not boil. Season to taste with salt and pepper and serve over oysters.

*T*he United States Naval Academy parking lot is the site of the world's largest crab feast. The annual event is sponsored by the Rotary Club and is held rain or shine. Last year, the event attracted over 3,000 crab lovers.

# Whitey's Red Hot Blue Crabs

1/2 cup seafood seasoning, piled high
1/4 cup plus 2 tablespoons coarse salt
3 tablespoons red pepper
3 tablespoons pickling spice
2 tablespoons celery seeds
1 tablespoon crushed red pepper
Water
Apple cider vinegar
12 blue crabs, alive and kicking

*Dipping Sauce:*
1/2 cup apple cider vinegar
1 tablespoon seafood seasoning

Combine first 6 ingredients; set aside.

Combine water and vinegar in equal amounts to a depth of 1 inch in a very large pot with a lid; bring to a boil. Place a rack in pot over boiling liquid; arrange half of crabs on rack. Sprinkle with half of the seasoning mixture. Top with remaining crabs and the rest of the seasoning mixture.

Cover tightly and steam 20 to 25 minutes, or until crabs turn bright red. Serve crabs hot or cold with beverage of your choice. Serves 4. For dipping sauce, combine ingredients.

*Serves 2 to 4.*

*Don't smash 'em, just crack 'em—a good crab knife is the secret to good crab picking. All over the Bay, this summer ritual is practiced. The picnic table is covered with brown butcher paper and the delicious and savory crabs are steamed a fiery red.*

*This crab picker decided she didn't want her photo taken, so she wrapped her head with paper towels. In commercial crab houses, crabs are steamed in large, cylindrical pots. They are then cooled and placed by the shovelful onto tables where they are picked and sorted by grade.*

# BALTIMORE CRAB CAKES

1 pound backfin crab meat

2 eggs, beaten lightly

2 tablespoons best quality mayonnaise

1 teaspoon prepared yellow mustard

2 slices day old bread, crusts removed

1 teaspoon Worcestershire sauce

1 teaspoon parsley

1/2 teaspoon Old Bay seasoning

Oil or butter for frying

Mix all ingredients except crab in large bowl. Add carefully picked
crab meat. Mix gently. Shape into cakes. Refrigerate for at least
1/2 hour (not necessary, but makes them much easier to fry).
Fry in a small amount of oil or butter until browned on each side.

*Serves 4 to 6.*

*For my first book, THE OFFICIAL CRAB
EATER'S GUIDE, I spent 5 years eating in
275 crab houses. That worked out to 3,000
crabs and a lot of beer. During that time, I
enjoyed hundreds of crab cakes and each
was different. This recipe is one that I've
enjoyed more than once.*

73

*Thomas Point Shoal offshore, 4 miles south of Annapolis.*

# LIGHTHOUSE CRAB IMPERIAL

**3 pounds backfin crab meat**

**1 green pepper, diced finely**

**1/2 jar red pimento, diced finely**

**1-1/2 teaspoon salt**

**1/2 teaspoon white pepper**

**2 raw eggs**

**1 cup mayonnaise**

**1 tablespoon dry mustard**

**Extra mayonnaise**

**Paprika**

Mix all ingredients except extra mayonnaise and paprika together and toss crab meat into the mixture last. Heap in crab shells or large casserole dish. Top with extra mayonnaise and paprika. Bake at 350 degrees for 20 minutes until top is brown. Serve hot or cold.

*Serves 12.*

*This is one of the easiest and tastiest casseroles you will ever fix, and, if you like crab imperial as much as I do, you'll probably end up fixing it several times a week. If anyone complains, and they shouldn't, I'll take the blame.*

*T*o be a keeper, a male crab must measure 5 inches point to point, a soft crab 3-1/2 inches, and a peeler 3 inches.

76

# CRAB MEAT AU GRATIN

2 tablespoons butter

2 tablespoons all-purpose flour

1-1/3 cups milk

1/2 teaspoon salt

1/8 teaspoon white pepper

1 pound crab meat

1/4 cup shredded mozzarella cheese

1/4 cup grated Parmesan cheese

1/4 cup soft bread crumbs

1/4 teaspoon paprika

Hot cooked rice

Melt butter in a heavy saucepan over low heat; add flour, stirring until smooth. Cook 1 minute, stirring constantly. Gradually add milk, cook over medium heat, stirring constantly, until thickened and bubbly. Stir in salt and pepper; stir in crab meat. Spoon seafood mixture into a lightly greased, 1 1/2-quart casserole. Bake at 350 degrees for 15 minutes. Combine cheeses, bread crumbs, and paprika, stirring well. Sprinkle over crab meat mixture, and bake an additional 3 minutes or until cheeses melt. Serve over rice.

*Serves 6.*

*When a dish is prepared au gratin, it usually means that the dish will be made with a crust across the top of grated cheese and bread crumbs and placed in an intense heat to cook. Our preparation differs very little from the general rule. You're going to love this recipe! I want you to try it tonight.*

"*It takes a lot of money to keep a boat like this up. There is always something breaking down and, Lord, the cost of everything has gone out of sight.*"

# Classic Crab Norfolk

**1 pound crab meat**

**2 tablespoons vinegar**

**1/2 teaspoon Tabasco sauce**

**1/2 teaspoon Worcestershire sauce**

**Salt to taste**

**Black pepper to taste**

**4 tablespoons melted butter**

Preheat oven to 350 degrees. Combine crab meat with vinegar, Tabasco sauce, Worcestershire sauce, salt, and pepper in a mixing bowl. Divide melted butter among four individual oven-proof serving dishes. Fill each dish with crab meat mixture and bake until very hot, about 15 minutes.

*Serves 4.*

*Classic crab Norfolk was created in 1924 by W. O. Snowden of the Snowden and Mason Restaurant in Norfolk, Virginia. This is the crowning touch to a festive holiday party, and you'll be proud to serve it to both your family and your most discriminating dinner guest. And if that isn't enough, it's easy to prepare.*

*T*he life cycle of the crab is no less enchant-
ing than the lifestyle of folks on the Bay.
Another Chesapeake specialty, soft shell
crabs, is available only when the crab
sheds, usually May through September.
A soft shell is a crab that has just molted, in
order to grow, and whose shell is not
hardened.

80

# STUFFED SOFT SHELL CRABS

**8 cleaned and dressed soft shell crabs**

**1/2 pound backfin crab meat**

**1/4 cup soft bread crumbs**

**1 egg, beaten**

**2 tablespoons mayonnaise**

**1/2 teaspoon dry mustard**

**1/2 teaspoon Worcestershire sauce**

**1/4 teaspoon salt**

**1/8 teaspoon pepper**

**All-purpose flour**

**Vegetable oil**

Wash crabs thoroughly; drain well. Remove any shell from crab meat. Combine crab meat and next seven ingredients; mix well. Stuff crab meat mixture evenly into cavity of each crab; dredge crabs in flour. Fry crabs in deep hot oil (375 degrees) for 1 to 2 minutes. Drain on paper towels; serve immediately.

*Serves 8.*

*Soft shells are graded and sold as "mediums," "hotels," and "primes." They are delicious and my favorite food either sauteed in butter or deep fried. Stuffing the soft crab is a wonderful variation on a theme. Forget about any side dishes—just serve this. It is a meal in itself.*

*L*ife along the Chesapeake waterway is
lined with crab floats as the watermen set
out from Smith Island, the heart of the Bay's
best crabbing grounds.

# CRAB LOUIS

**1 small head lettuce**
**1 pound jumbo lump crab meat**
**4 hard-cooked eggs**
**2 tomatoes, quartered**
**1 medium cucumber, sliced**

***Louis Dressing:***
**1/3 cup mayonnaise**
**1/2 cup bottled chili sauce**
**2 tablespoons French dressing**
**1/2 teaspoon minced onion**
**1/2 teaspoon Worcestershire sauce**
**Salt and pepper**

Mix dressing ingredients until blended (makes about 1 cup).
Place shredded lettuce on salad plate. Top with crab meat.
Garnish with egg, tomato, and cucumber. Serve with Louis dressing.

*Serves 4.*

*Smith Islanders are particular about crab salad and rightly so. Crabs are their life. For the total effect of this dish, use only freshly picked jumbo lump crab meat. I promise you that this recipe will be one of your all-time favorites.*

*W*hen the day's fishing is done, the work has just begun.

# LOWER BAY
# BAKED SEA TROUT

**1 to 1-1/4 pound sea trout fillet**

**4 cleaned mussels**

**4 onion slices**

**4 fresh tomato slices**

**4 green pepper rings**

**4 sprigs fresh thyme**

**4 sprigs fresh sage**

**2 crushed white peppercorns**

**Melted butter**

**White wine**

Divide the fish into two equal portions and place skinned side down on parchment paper. Garnish the fish with onion slices, tomato slices, and thin pepper rings. Place the mussels on top and then the herbs and pepper. Drizzle a little melted butter and wine on the fish and then seal the paper parchment, twisting the ends well. Coat the outside with additional melted butter and bake at 350 degrees for about 20 minutes.

*Serves 2.*

*Wrapping delicate food such as sea trout in paper parcels is an inventive way of ensuring that all the flavors remain sealed in. For full effect, open the parcels at the table. There is a whole world of flavor in this dish. I want you to try it and see if you don't agree!*

*It was a spring like no other. We sat on the river bank and watched the action. It didn't take long for the bucket to fill. We traded a print of this photo for fish.*

# FANTASTIC BAKED FLOUNDER

**1-pound fish fillets, 1-inch thick, cut into serving-size pieces**
**2 tablespoons yellow cornmeal**
**2 tablespoons flour**
**1/4 teaspoon paprika**
**Salt and pepper**
**1 tablespoon oil**
**1 tablespoon grated Parmesan cheese**

Pat fish dry with paper towels. Combine cornmeal, flour, paprika, and a dash each of salt and pepper in a flat dish. Place oil in baking dish; heat in 425 degree oven for 1 minute. Dredge fish in cornmeal mixture; shake off excess. Place in baking dish and turn to coat with oil. Arrange fish pieces 1 inch apart. Sprinkle with Parmesan cheese. Bake at 425 degrees for 10 minutes. Fish flakes when tested with a fork.

*Serves 4.*

*Although most folks first associate crabs with the Bay, another creature has vied for the culinary attention with pleasant results. Give this tantalizing flounder a try. It's delightful.*

*M*any call the Chesapeake Bay, "the best fishing hole in America." Among its best-known fish are rockfish, sea trout, croakers, Norfolk spot, bluefish, black drum, catfish, flounder, and yellow and white perch. This photograph shows pound trap net fishermen loading their catch.

# POCOMOKE SOUND GRILLED BLUEFISH

**2 large bluefish fillets, with skin**

*Marinade:*
**1/2 cup fresh lime juice**

**1 teaspoon grated lime rind**

**3 cloves garlic, crushed**

**1/2 cup olive oil**

**2 teaspoons minced fresh ginger**

**Salt and pepper**

Mix the marinade ingredients together and pour over the bluefish fillets in a shallow dish. Turn to coat both sides well and cover. Marinate for 3 hours in the refrigerator. On hot charcoal or in a preheated gas grill, cook the flesh side of the fillet first for approximately 6 minutes, or until the fish is lightly browned. Turn over and baste the fish well with the marinade. Grill the skin side an additional 3 to 5 minutes, or until the fish is thoroughly cooked. Reheat the marinade and transfer the fish to a hot serving platter. Pour the remaining marinade over the fish to serve.

*Serves 6.*

*Here is yet another recipe for this popular fish, but this time in a slightly different style. Besides adding flavor to this fish, the marinade helps to keep it moist while grilling. All you do is follow this recipe to the letter and you've got yourself a winner.*

*Chesapeake stripers are back!*

# BAKED ROCKFISH WITH CRAB MEAT STUFFING

1/3 cup minced onion

3 tablespoons butter

1/2 pound crab meat

1/2 cup fresh bread crumbs

1/4 cup fresh chopped parsley

1/4 cup heavy cream

1 teaspoon lemon thyme

4-pound striped bass, dressed for stuffing

Salt and pepper

1/3 cup dry white wine mixed with 1/3 cup melted butter

Saute onion in butter until golden. Remove from heat and mix in the crab meat, bread crumbs, parsley, heavy cream, and lemon thyme. Sprinkle cavity of fish lightly with salt and pepper. Stuff the fish and skewer edges securely. Place fish in a greased baking pan and pour wine-butter mixture over fish. Bake in 400-degree oven, uncovered for 30 minutes, or just until the flesh is opaque, basting frequently with wine sauce.

*Serves 4 to 6.*

*Now that the tasty "Rockfish" is back, here's a great way to prepare your catch. This dish makes an elegant entree or a lazy day porch supper when company's coming. I promise it'll get you rave reviews!*

*T*his photograph, taken in Warsaw, Virginia, shows a fisherman unloading the day's catch. This happens to be bait fish that will be used to stock crab pots.

# BEER BATTER FRIED FISH

2/3 cup flour

1/3 cup corn starch

1/2 cup water

1/2 cup beer

1 teaspoon pepper

1 tablespoon oil

1 tablespoon baking powder

1 teaspoon salt

Peanut oil for frying

1/2 pound pan-dressed fish fillets, per person

In a medium bowl, combine all the ingredients and mix well. Dip fillets into batter and fry in hot oil until golden brown.

*Serves 4.*

*The flavor of fish is at its peak when dipped in this delightful beer batter and fried to a rich, golden brown. I suggest you serve fried fish with a creamed vegetable, baked potato, tossed green salad, and, of course, a bottle of chilled white wine to sip between bites.*

# Desserts

# BANANA BREAD

1/2 cup butter

3/4 cup light brown sugar

1 cup mashed bananas

2 eggs

1 teaspoon salt

1-1/2 cups flour

1 teaspoon baking soda

1/2 cup milk

1/2 cup chopped nuts

Cream the butter with sugar. Add the mashed bananas and eggs. Sift the flour with salt and baking soda and add to the creamed mixture alternately with the milk. Stir in the nuts. Bake in a greased loaf pan 8-1/2 x 4-1/2 x 2-1/2 inches in a 350 degree oven for an hour. Turn out and cool on rack.

*Serves 6.*

*Mom always said, "This bread is better the second day." With 14 little mouths to feed, I wonder how she knew that.*

*Sailboat races on the Chesapeake Bay are a familiar sight.*

# OLD FASHIONED PINEAPPLE UPSIDE-DOWN CAKE

3 cans sliced pineapple (8-1/4 ounces) in heavy syrup (12 slices)
1/4 cup butter
2/3 cup light brown sugar
1/3 cup pecan halves
1 cup unsifted all-purpose flour
3/4 cup granulated sugar
1-1/2 teaspoons baking powder

1/2 teaspoon salt
1/4 cup shortening
1/2 cup milk
1 egg
1 cup heavy cream, chilled

Preheat oven to 350 degrees. Drain pineapple slices, reserving 2 tablespoons of the syrup. In a very heavy, or iron, 10-inch skillet with heat-resistant handle, melt butter over medium heat. Add brown sugar, stirring until sugar is melted. Remove from heat. Arrange 8 pineapple slices on sugar mixture, overlapping slices slightly around edge of pan. Put one slice in center. Fill centers with pecan halves. Halve three remaining pineapple slices. Arrange around inside edge of skillet. Put pecans in centers.

In medium bowl, sift flour with granulated sugar, baking powder, and salt. Add shortening and milk. With electric mixer at high speed, beat 2 minutes, or until mixture is smooth. Add egg and reserved 2 tablespoons pineapple syrup; beat 2 minutes longer. Gently pour cake batter over pineapple in skillet, spreading even-ly, being careful not to disarrange pineapple. On rack in center of oven, bake 40 to 45 minutes, or until golden in color and surface of cake springs back when it is gently pressed with fingertip.

Let skillet stand on wire rack 5 minutes to cool just slightly. With rotary beater, beat cream until stiff. With small spatula, loosen cake from edge of skillet all around. Place serving platter over the cake, turn upside down, shake gently, and lift off skillet. Serve cake warm with the whipped cream.

*Serves 8.*

*U*p in the big house, down in the kitchen,
come boys, come boys, let's go fishin', and
give Mama time to bake this pumpkin pie.

98

# POINT LOOKOUT PUMPKIN PIE

**2 cups cooked pumpkin (fresh or canned)**
**2 beaten eggs**
**1 cup brown sugar**
**1 cup half-and-half**
**1/2 cup milk**
**1 tablespoon brandy**
**1 teaspoon vanilla extract**
**1 teaspoon cinnamon**
**1 teaspoon ground ginger**
**1/2 teaspoon allspice**
**1 9-inch pie crust**
**1 cup whipping cream**

Preheat oven to 425 degrees. Stir together pumpkin and eggs. Then stir in sugar, half-and-half, milk, and brandy. Add remaining flavorings and stir well. Use a 9-inch pie plate and line plate with dough, gently pressing it into bottom and sides. Spoon pumpkin filling into pie shell and spread evenly. Bake pie for 15 minutes. Reduce oven temperature to 350 degrees and bake for 20 to 25 minutes more, until a thin knife blade inserted into the filling comes out clean. Let pie cool to room temperature. Whip cream and spoon generously over pie before serving.

*Serves 6.*

*In earlier times, this pie would have been called a pudding. Spices were not included, though, until the clipper ships began their trade. Squash is often used as an alternative ingredient, but whichever you choose, Thanksgiving would not be the same without it. Why wait for a holiday to happen!*

*A*utumn is the perfect time for bird watching. Canadian geese arrive in large numbers, as well as 40 other species in all, to splash down in the mild, homey waters of the Chesapeake Bay and begin their winter roost.

# LEMON TEA BREAD

**3/4 cup milk**
**1 tablespoon finely chopped lemon balm**
**1 tablespoon finely chopped lemon thyme**
**2 cups all-purpose flour**
**1-1/2 teaspoons baking powder**
**1/4 teaspoon salt**
**6 tablespoons butter, at room temperature**
**1 cup sugar**
**2 eggs, beaten separately**
**1 tablespoon grated lemon zest**

Butter a 9 x 5 x 3-inch pan. Preheat the oven to 325 degrees. Heat the milk with the chopped herbs and let steep until cool.

Mix the flour, baking powder, and salt together in a bowl. In another bowl, cream the butter and gradually beat in the sugar. Continue beating until light and fluffy. Beat in the eggs, one at a time. Beat in the lemon zest. Add the flour mixture alternately with the herbed milk. Mix until the batter is just blended. Put the batter into the prepared pan. Bake for about 50 minutes, or until a toothpick inserted in the center comes out dry. Remove from the pan onto a wire rack that is set over a sheet of waxed paper. Pour Lemon Glaze over the still-hot bread. Decorate with a few sprigs of lemon thyme.

*Serves 8.*

*Lemon Glaze:*
**Juice of 1 lemon**
**Confectioners sugar**

Put the lemon juice in a bowl and add the sugar, stirring until a thick but still pourable paste forms. Pour the glaze over the hot bread.

*Now here's a bread that will stick with you all day long. Serve it with tea for breakfast. It's so good, in fact, I wouldn't be suprised if you served it for lunch, dinner, or even a late night snack.*

*P*ractically any part of the Chesapeake and
its country has something of interest for the
artist and the photographer, but in my esti-
mation, Smith Island has more atmosphere.

# CLASSIC BREAD PUDDING

**4 slices stale bread, preferably whole-wheat**

**2 tablespoons butter**

**1/2 cup raisins**

**1/4 teaspoon cinnamon**

**1/4 teaspoon nutmeg**

**3 eggs lightly beaten**

**1/3 cup sugar**

**1-1/4 cups milk**

Spread butter on each slice of bread and cut in cubes. Place half the cubes on bottom of a 1-1/2 to 2-quart casserole dish that has been sprayed with non-stick coating. Sprinkle half the raisins and half the spices over bread. Top with remaining bread cubes, raisins, and spices.

Place eggs in bowl and beat with sugar until light. Add milk, mix, and pour over bread cubes. Let stand for at least an hour. About 25 or 30 minutes before you plan to bake pudding, preheat oven to 350 degrees. Place casserole in a pan big enough to hold it and enough warm water to come halfway up sides of baking dish.

Bake for about an hour or until mixture is set and does not coat knife inserted in its middle. Serve slightly warm or cold.

*Serves 6 to 8.*

*The true sense of the word—classic—indeed, being a model of its kind of the highest class. The simplicity of this dish says it all.*

*B*lackberry cobbler is my all-time, child-
hood, favorite dessert. Memories remain of
riding bikes to our secret picking patch,
putting on protective clothing, and grab-
bing a bucket or saucepan—anything that
would hold plenty of berries. You might
have gotten scratches from the thorny
bushes, but the reward came when Mom
made her delicious cobbler.

# Mom's Southern Blackberry Cobbler

**3 cups fresh blackberries**
**About 3/4 cup sugar**
**3 tablespoons all-purpose flour**
**1-1/2 cups water**
**1 tablespoon lemon juice**
**Crust (recipe follows)**
**2 tablespoons butter, melted**

Place berries in a lightly greased shallow 2-quart baking dish. Combine sugar and flour; stir in water and lemon juice. Pour mixture over berries, and bake at 425 degrees for 15 minutes. Place crust over hot berries and brush with butter. Bake at 425 degrees for 20 to 30 minutes or until crust is golden brown.

*Serves 8.*

***Crust:***
**1-3/4 cups all-purpose flour**
**2 teaspoons baking powder**
**3/4 teaspoon salt**
**2 to 3 tablespoons sugar**
**1/4 cup shortening**
**1/4 cup plus 2 tablespoons whipping cream**
**1/4 cup plus 2 tablespoons buttermilk**

Combine first four ingredients. Cut in shortening with pastry blender until mixture resembles coarse meal; stir in whipping cream and buttermilk. Knead dough four or five times; roll out on a lightly floured surface. Cut dough to fit baking dish.

*Who can resist warm blackberry cobbler, one of the nicest things to happen to fresh blackberries. The amount of sugar to add in this recipe is determined by the sweetness of the berries.*

*The first settlers of Virginia proclaimed the land full of "fine and beautiful strawberries, four times bigger and better than ours in England..." (from the narrative of Captain George Perce, April 26, 1607).*

# STRAWBERRY SHORTCAKE

2 cups sifted all-purpose flour
1/4 cup granulated sugar
3 teaspoons baking powder
1/2 teaspoon salt
1/2 cup butter, cut into chunks
1 egg
Milk
2 tablespoons butter, melted

*Topping:*
2 pint boxes fresh
    strawberries
1/2 cup granulated sugar
1 cup heavy cream
2 tablespoons
    confectioners sugar

Wash berries in cold water; drain. Set aside several nice ones for garnish. Remove hulls from rest of berries; slice half of berries into bowl; toss with 1/4 cup granulated sugar. With fork, crush other half of berries with 1/4 cup sugar.

With portable electric mixer, beat cream with confectioners sugar just until stiff; refrigerate.

With sifter placed in medium bowl, sift flour with 1/4 cup granulated sugar, the baking powder, and salt. With pastry blender, cut 1/2 cup butter into flour mixture until it is in very small particles, each coated with flour (resembles small peas). Break egg into a 1-cup measuring cup. Add milk to measure 3/4 cup. Mix with fork. Make well in center of flour mixture. Pour in milk-egg mixture all at once; mix vigorously with fork until moistened.

Lightly grease an 8 x 1-1/2 inch round, layer cake pan. Turn dough into prepared pan, scraping bowl with rubber scraper. With the rubber scraper, smooth top of dough so that it is even in pan.

Bake 25 to 30 minutes at 425 degrees, or until golden, and cake tester inserted in center comes out clean. Loosen edge with sharp knife; turn out on a wire rack. Using a long, serrated knife, cut cake in half crosswise. Place bottom of cake, cut side up, on serving plate. Brush surface with melted butter. Spoon on half of crushed and sliced berries; set top in place, cut side down. Spoon on rest of berries. Mound whipped cream lightly in center. Garnish with whole berries. Serve warm, in wedges.

*Serves 9.*

*P*ictured here are Navy yachtsmen engaged in a traditional fall race held annually near Annapolis, Maryland. This dramatic print was taken in the early evening hours using infrared film.

# LADY BALTIMORE CAKE

| 1 cup butter | 2 teaspoons cream of tartar |
|---|---|
| 1-3/4 cups sugar | 1/2 teaspoon nutmeg |
| 7 egg yolks, large | 1 teaspoon baking soda |
| 3 cups flour | 1 cup milk |
| 1/4 teaspoon salt | 1/2 teaspoon lemon flavoring |

Cream butter and sugar until light and fluffy. Add egg yolks, one at a time, and beat until smooth. Sift the dry ingredients together. Add to egg mixture alternately with milk and lemon flavoring. Pour into two 9-inch pans lined with waxed paper, and bake in a 350-degree oven for 30 to 40 minutes. Spread fruit-nut frosting between layers and on top and sides of cake after cake has cooled.

*Frosting:*

| | 1 teaspoon vanilla |
|---|---|
| 3 egg whites | 1/4 cup candied cherries |
| 1-1/8 cups sugar | 1/4 cup seedless raisins |
| 1/4 cup light rum | 1/2 cup walnuts, chopped |
| 1/2 teaspoon cream of tartar | |
| Pinch salt | |

Mix the egg whites, sugar, rum, cream of tartar, and salt in the top part of a double boiler over boiling water. Beat continuously for about 7 minutes until the mixture stands in peaks when the batter is lifted and turned up. Remove from the heat. When cool, add vanilla, cherries, raisins, and walnuts. Spread generously over the top, middle, and sides of cake. Decorate rim with additional walnut halves.

*Serves 8 to 10.*

*There are a great many stories that go with this marvelous cake. For one, it was said to have originated with the first Lord Baltimore and his wife. It has also been associated with an owner of a Charleston, South Carolina restaurant, the Lady Baltimore Tea Room. Novelist, Owen Wister, regularly had tea and cake here, and he borrowed the name of the restaurant for his 1906 romance novel, LADY BALTIMORE.*

109

# Recipe Index

## About the Author

**Whitey Schmidt**, a native Marylander who lives on "the Bay," is author of the popular culinary classic–THE CRAB COOKBOOK–published in 1990. Schmidt has sampled Chesapeake cuisine for over 25 years, visiting more than 425 of the region's eateries including waterfront seafood establishments and crab houses. Other Schmidt selections include A GUIDE TO CHESAPEAKE SEAFOOD DINING–BAYSIDE VIEWS TO DINE BY and the best-selling THE OFFICIAL CRAB EATER'S GUIDE. The food writer's thoughts on fine dining and tempting meal preparation appear regularly in his weekly The *Voice of Southern Maryland* column– "Schmidt's Hits," in *Bay Sailor* magazine restaurant reviews, in various other Chesapeake Bay publications, as well as on radio shows around "the Bay."

## About the Photographer

**Marion E. Warren**, has been capturing the mood and beauty of the Chesapeake since 1947, when he left St. Louis where he had worked as as Associated Press photographer. Images created by Warren have appeared in six previous books. The White House, the U.S. Navy, the State of Maryland, and the Smithsonian have been named on his impressive client list. Warren has donated 100,000 negatives and prints of his life's work to the Maryland State Archives. He is currently working on a comprehensive Chesapeake Bay photo book in cooperation with Johns Hopkins University.

# Acknowledgements

Mike Dirham

Falcon Color, Inc.

Falls Camera

Bob Hammond

Louise Jennings

Robin Quinn

Tab Distributing Company

Capt. Larry Thomas

Tom Vernon

Tony Vernon

Cover design and book production by Denise McDonald

For additional information on ordering books or discount schedule, write:

Marian Hartnett Press
Box 51
Friendship Rd.
Friendship, Maryland 20758